D1084650

THE APPARITIONERS

THREE RAIL PRESS / SEATTLE

....

....

....

....

....

THE APPARITIONERS / GEORGE WITTE

CONTENTS

FOR MY MOTHER

Eva Merrill Witte

THE APPARITIONERS

AN OPEN LETTER

There's something to be said
for sitting still and letting things come clear,
the way morning fog burns off the lake.

A friend writes: enlisted
in the Air Force, put on weight and saw the world
you missed. I'm content
to wait on what drops by
or swoops in for a closer view.
My doors are open wide, windows propped
so wind feels free
to flip through my mail, discarding
bills and funeral notices,
scattering pale
handwritten pages on the lawn for everyone
to read. A wedding invitation
went to buttress an oriole nest;
one man passing on the road nearby
pulled over, furtively stuffed a single
sheet in his back pocket, then drove along;
and the last I saw
my friend's letter held its own
with the wind, lightly at tree level

like the jet he flies far
and high away from here.

There's something to be said, and something else
to be kept quiet and cool:
the lake at dawn, before the fog burns off.

For months on end we had no rain.
The weekends wheeled by, spokes around
A parching sun that flung off light,
Satellite of drought transmitting
To our state. No one seemed to care—
Terrific day! was the watchword—
And while whole forests burned to ash
We watered our lawns, secretly
At night against the governor's
Decree, sprinklers drawing their fronds
Like pale girls in prom gowns over
Cool thick grass.
                      Lake levels slipped low;
We saw the bed for the first time
In years, how filthy it had gone
In the polluted interim.
A pall of muck, the drifted ash,
Clotted tires and matchbooks,
Stopped the mouth of an odd beer can
From gurgling its jingle and fouled
The bottom springs that fed the lake.

It became a pastime, looking
In: we saw these things through faces,

Ours, spread over them like clear shrouds
Preserving shapes as they decayed.
Three deep along the shore or poling
Out in longboats, our reflections
Vanished into fissures when the sun
Hit high noon and stayed, crackling dry
The lake, and our fair state became
A country of perfect weekends
Where no one traveled or complained.
Standing in shadows, to each his own,
We hunch like water birds above
The hacked lake bed, searching for us.

Fossilized in moss, siding soft
With furze, the wellhouse leans one nail's-
   Breadth from collapse above
     The covered well.
    A narrow undercroft
Delves twenty feet through stone to mine
The water table's lowest plane;
   Whoever dug it tapped
     A virgin vein
   Long concealed, artesian,
That flows through drought, an undertow
Of pure desire. Nearby, a wall
   Piled from loose rock proclaims
     An owner's bill:
   This side is mine to sow.
The rest is wilderness. No home
In evidence; the foundation
   Sways with ferns, broad mushrooms.
     A dream fell in
   Here like a sinkhole's yawn
Leached in lime, gulping paradise
Whole. Innately fertile, the well
   Fills to overflow,
     Available

Manna for passersby.
I duck inside the rotted hull,
Cup hands into the ring of stone,
　　Taste: an image rises:
　　　A man alone
　　Hammers a cathedral
Up from boards to house the cold wound
Of his longing, and rakes it clear
　　Of leaves and swollen toads,
　　　The well the core
　　His life revolves around,
And sees his calm reflection choose
Its own level in the rainfall's
　　Ebb and seep each season,
　　　And learns the full,
　　Inviolate repose
Of the thing, anything at all.

By my daughter's bedside light I read
myself into fear, though I am her protector.
A schoolmate died—a boy, the cause unclear.
Thinking to provide comfort to the class
the teacher made a tale of it, where angels
hovered down to steal him while he slept.
Now parents across town keep vigilant
until our children rest, come running when
they wake to find themselves abandoned
to their common nightmare, the thrum of wings.

Can reading up on horror summon it?
My book describes a man, trapped in debt
and made sick by God, who killed his own—
mother, wife, three children—left his church a note,
then disappeared. Our suburban Eden's
Hell for some; my ex-wife knew a woman
who cut her throat while watching in the glass,
as if death unwitnessed would go ignored.
We groom the wilderness to demark space,
the border you don't want to violate.

Yet some trespass without fear: cats step light
from lawn to lawn, never looking down.
At night our dreams glow white as negatives

where shadows mass into a door through which
the gone return, to wander restlessly
like shoppers in a mall they can't afford.
We frighten children with our fantasies;
when one coheres we abdicate the watch,
leave our nightmare to the kids—or them to it.
Our no-man's land is its dominion.

So when one child cries at night, the others
echo, like dogs announcing an intruder.
Their parents' lights click on to ease the dark;
next day we greet each other at the train,
or downtown running errands—rheumy-eyed
survivors wired on coffee, cigarettes.
When my daughter wakes, asking for her mom,
I tell her she's not with us anymore.
Who's she with? I don't know—she disappeared.
On that she sleeps and I take up my book.

A wind arrives to scour the yard's few trees.
Branch tips snap, deep roots pop as if rough hands
gripped to yank them from their anchorage.
Here we are safe—my book's no conjure thing,
my daughter sleeps untroubled by its spell,
her animals arrayed to guard the bed.
But in another home, the angels' stealth
won't be resisted: a child awakens
fevered in the dark, his parents gone, to know
a bristling wing placed frankly on his brow.

STRAYS

In nondescript cars of uncertain make
anonymous monsters arrive and go,
glide quiet past schoolyards, apply the brake.

They've read all our seminal books and know
which children will follow, which run away,
how witnesses secret behind windows

report tomorrow who's missing today.
By then the path's cold, visible contrail
erasing itself before memory—

sour musty cologne, aroma of oil,
face no one can finger, name on tongue's end
never told. We pray for a miracle,

milk carton photo made flesh, child returned
to play in some neighborhood's paradise.
We melt candles, allow porchlights to burn,

inquisitors testing our alibis,
attract small furred moths that flutter and shake
in subtle webs architectured nearby,

stray husks bound and collected come daybreak.

Silence silences; snow turns down its bed-
sheet, beckoning the body into rest.
No bird calls another, no animal's
yet tracked across the field you breathe beneath.
That this would last, the climate hold a while—
your prayer—is answered by the snowplow's rasp
on asphalt, the clock's alarum, the give
and take antiphony of garbagemen
cursing out the weather you awake in.
Get up. Music pipes from nowhere, lone wind
instrument to greet the sun, saxophone
for urban settings, countryside a flute.
Small stirrings inspire riffs to mimic them:
the mouse that peeks above the snow a trill
ascending, hawk that circles it dread chord
the camera seems to tremble from.

                                       Your heart
has come to crave this muscle tug, or else
you would not know to feel or what to see.
To laugh you need familiar laughter, live
or taped, the track invisible that gives
permission to respond. You listen for
the voiceover, its promised intimates—
haunt and habitat, predator and prey

to stalk your days, lend drama to routine.
This silence plucks your thready nerves, the way
a gap in conversation opens doors
you slam shut briskly with a joke. The snow's
voice is itself, soundlessly explaining
why and how it visits earth, a purpose
cloaking all it brushes, collecting weight.
You cannot understand a thing it says.

THAW

The county ponds still blind
With icy cataracts,
I walked the ridge's spine
Where trees smashed cold-cast
Skins of glass and towered
Wet above the wreckage.
My eyes' ironic squint
Unlocked by picks of light,
A glint made intricate
By motion drew me near;
A web between two limbs,
Invisible at ease,
Flexed just above my head,
Its lower half a mine
Of gnats englobed in dew.
I turned: the ridge entire
Bridged delicate with them,
Dripped, steamed, glittered and cracked,
Rare instrument whose strings
Trembled from connection,
Whose pitch was breath's, whose fires
Your merest touch ignites.

TALUS SLOPE

Buckled up by continental
Grind so slow and powerful it
Fused frail-boned fossils of an age
Long dead into an iron spine,
The ridge juts black against the rain,
Holding nothing back. Striations
In the stone mark a glacier's till
Of retreat; the thick cold tongue stripped
Topsoil neat like skin, exposing
Sheer cliffs.
                This winter, as always,
Rain and snow slip like simple words
Into the cracks of rhetoric
And swell a little. Ice crystals
Sprout perpendicular to ground,
Infinite delicate chisels
Chip the cliff face out until it
Collapses into stone strewn clean
Down-mountain like a river bed
Gone arid.
                But tilt a boulder
On the slope, bend close: a single
Crystal hardens like a bud dew-
Wet with origins, hieroglyph

Of a secret life. At dawn or
After rain, or beneath calm drifts
Of snow, the ridge is blossoming
Within itself, its shales peel off
Like petals to reveal the peak
Of rock, the heart learning to speak.

Bronze and silver, hammered gold, turquoise, flint.
Arrows mounted beside guns.
Teeth under glass,
a chief's, largesse of the government
pried back from his corpse. Feathers,
as if some pinioned thing just flown
had scattered them, broken by imprisonment
but free. The brochure shone,
full-color, lavishly produced,
collector's item worth the price. The dead
lived up to their eulogy;
brave but futile deeds rehearsed
with conqueror's humility, a touch
it must have taken drafts to hone.

We'd driven cross-
country for these relics, witnesses
to crimes we couldn't recognize as such
in the curated afterlife where war's
nostalgia, genocide a myth
the victims play for sympathy.
Our parents hoped it educational.
Dad strode forward as if gulled
by ghosts panhandling history,

not looking back. My brother and I
wished ourselves warriors, merciless
as shadows cast by cliffs at sunset
spreading toward the plain where wagons slept,
girls and women begging to be scalped.
(We teased our sister, whose hair was sacrosanct.)
The sky lit lurid red
meant something big, a secret code
the painter's palette hid, or so the brochure said.

My mother lingered, seeming lost,
like she'd found the aisle but forgot
her shopping list. Uniformed guards
harassed her: *Can I help you, miss?*
She must have looked suspicious,
thief or nutcase, mumbling to herself
before the reconstructed grave, typed cards
explaining this or that symbolic shard,
a miserly hoard which bored us.
Scanning shelves of unmade artifacts
her eyes teared bright and hard.
What's wrong with you? I whispered fierce,
embarrassed. As if slapped
she stiffened, examining my face
with a doctor's eye for symptoms.
Nothing's wrong, she snapped.
Don't you ever talk to me like that.

Above us, great lopped-off heads
of extinct gods leaned down to eavesdrop.
Tanned skins rippled on their nails.
The copper horseman leapt before the snake,
wild-eyed bison pinwheeled off the cliff.
Like the wind over the earth he will come.

This hand spread and closed
four strokes, a square
defining your absence
like a home's foundation left
unfinished, the blueprint's scroll
a text too frail
for light to touch, to read by.
From the stone of these words
no angel rose, ethereal or carved;
no afterimage lingered in the eye
when we blinked and found you gone
though strangers seemed familiar
for a time, as if the living like a shroud
assumed the features of the dead.

Those recognitions passed.
Faces of an alien cast
rang down with the glare of visors,
each guarding his own passion,
perhaps disfigured by it, and ashamed,
perhaps unwilling to relinquish it,
a secret hump that feeds
upon us, as it devoured you.
Years later, this talisman

flutters from a drawer—
age, the church that buried you, kin whose names
summon, like an echo, yours—
and the hand that clipped your elegy
now cradles it, yellow as a leaf
pressed between the pages of a book,
the plot abandoned while
different ends were possible.

In the Flatbrook's surly
Ease of motion, a swaggering:
    Contours test stone's patience,
Swing wide to undercut an oak
    Or sieve through rapids' teeth,
Reforming into pools downstream.
    Three levels emerge, first
The surface flow, a glittering
    Roil slowed by obstructions.
Fallen branches mark a thicket's
    Argument, contradict
The course of common sense, the least
    Resistant path brooks take.
Less ambiguous, the under-
    Current trues blue water
Against the bank, velocity
    A constant. High in spring
With melt, the surface can deceive,
    Seem sluggish; this level
Sweeps its cold corridor all year.
    At the deepest structure
The brook is still. A thermocline
    Defines the temperate

Zone between the upper water
    And here, the monarchy
Of trout. At dusk, the pool holds light's
    Refraction like a lens,
Their shadows mass, they rise to feed,
    Motion's sense is rendered
Up, the brook's alphabet inscribed.

GULLY

Small things bring small consequences.
A stone nudged from its set doesn't
matter, much—still, this one's shape was

odd, concave, fluted at the rim
so snow melt flowed to either side
or pooled in the smooth declension.

Over time a delta opened
below the stone where water sieved,
but slow enough for soil to tend

a modest garden, one spider
presiding over small domain,
caretaker of husks and dew-stars,

these shrubs whose roots now gleam like bone
exposed, phlox slicked dead as blue hair,
web that limned a constellation

torn, for the stone nudged from its set
divides the mountain, carves a line
to mark its absence like a ghost's

initial, who will never rest again.

On wing's edge, phalanges
Quilled like troops to battle
Branch from bone, structuring
A monument. Aloft
Each feather filtered wind's
Component speeds to glide
Inviolate over
Hill, skim the mountain ridge.
Now the pinion's shackled,
Stripped to bristle, hollow
Shell whose cells remember
Flight's echoic language,
Frail correspondences
Required of mass and air
To lift the hawk into
Orbit, inscribe its arc.
Turning heart of the world,
Whirl's king, you ruled the field
Objectively—two wheels
In synch as one—then fell.
The pure mechanics stilled;
Entropy, then stasis.
Combed bone. Imagining

Your orrery, the mind
Clicks planets into place,
The center grips, oiled gears
Grind alive, their cogs catch
And mesh: the world spins new.

SPOILS

The fields near ours sprout crops of signs:

FOR SALE   WARNING

ZONED BUSINESS   NO TRESPASS

A bier of bottles marks a bristling X
that whistles lowdown when the wind picks up.
Someone's blacked out ZDBUESS and TRESP,
embellishing what's left with art:
a woman raped three ways at once, her sex
carved intricate as if to prove
the special knowledge of the scribe in love,
each detail a bloody rampart
stormed in dream—a monk's illumination.

Like a swimmer parting fog before me
I follow corn rows bright with rain
past the scattered ruins of the boom
that echoed out: the billboard cons
where smiling humans grazed the Shoppes and skied
peel down in frail fronds, the mall's foundation
a dolmen of cement and rust.
The highway spur they sold us on now dead-
ends, trestle spine a broken aqueduct.

I come to barbed wire, landsman's stand,
more gesture than enforcement, for
the strands sag loose, cradle buckled fenceposts
like wives their beaten men.
A red glint flags me down:
a ring of flannel sleeve torn clean
dangles from the wire, beacon in the fog.
I disengage it, polish crosshatched threads—
blue and grey, with hard flecks of red
that might be mud, or paint, or blood,
impossible to tell—and see
a traveler, striding across
fields and fences through a homeland plundered
beyond recognition, his gait so fierce
he cannot pause when some tooth tugs his arm
but rips it free, not looking back,
for where he's headed there are shirts to burn,
fire to consume them, and no one
left to miss or mend the banner
he's abandoned, that scalds my pocket now.

OCTOBER ROSE

October rose, around you
sparrows whirl through fall's
false spring, the spell that licked you open
nipping them to nervous
swerves and halts, stutter-
step disturbances
beneath damp trees whose limbs
the wind will comb.
              Survivor of the frost's
first brittle shear, your hue
clean startles from the killing ground—
sunflowers matted down like hair,
the sere forsythia, the pricker's
bony buttress—as if a casket lid
slammed open to reveal
the vampire's lips: just moistened, pink and full.
                       A bee

with you awakened by a clement breeze
mines the folded mysteries
of your core, lingering
over outer petals, until
the promise of your taste—
the buried fire of succulence—
returns its kiss.

Yet come morning
dew, your lover warm in the hive,
sparrows circling southward and dry leaves
strewn like garments on the lawn,
the flame you stayed them with
lasts only in these lines' rekindled pyre.

TO BE OPENED IN THE EVENT

The crispnesses of autumn: new
picked apples bitten into,
white corn shucked and boiled, squash split,
tactile crunch of acorns underfoot,
summer's hiss and drone
hushed out when rime's fresh chill
brittles the cathedral.
Easy to be sentimental—
The season sure flew by, where
does time go?—to contrive
a companionable shiver
the flare of urgent signs can't scare,
your place amid the whirl and burn
secure, bought and paid for
(more or less): the silent punch line
your crowd anticipates with grins.
Summer's re-rehearsed in semaphore,
rifts and sly alliances
concealed by fellowship's
cartoon, a beery stir
of out-of-focus sin made funny
with exaggeration. *All lies*, one says,
naming common ground.

A toast, artfully designed
to mock, but flatter, and bless at last
the turning's genius and its host;
then one by one guests back away
like minor characters exiting a play
with gestures to recall them by—
an ironic bow, a wink, loud laughter
at the threshold—and though their ghosts
may linger late for one last drink
these too in time disperse, the closets
groan with coats forgotten
in farewell, the crystal whispers low,
and remnant sparrows glean the lawn
for pickings of discarded rind
whose fruit now sours your tongue
with the aftertaste of ash.
                              So long.

HALLOWEEN

Corn rows stripped to husk and fibrous gristle.
Crows rake with appetites no chaff can slake,
ragged priests chittering queer eulogy,
mist above the grave. Heads bowed, lingering
thoughtful before pumpkins, we seem to mourn
or pray such ripeness might inhabit us.
We choose a skull to light our patio.

Suddenly all birds rise in one body,
shadow and original together
flowing over fields toward the orchard,
trees in silhouette like buried fingers
gnarling upward, as if they grasped for souls.
Presence in the air, tang of snow and fire:
char and turn our rinds that we may flower.

That day gave way, each ledge of light
eroding into sparks damp grass
absorbed, a whispered hiss beneath
the calls of dogs and kids: Goodnight.
Fireflies flashed their signal language
here and there, one syllable (pause)
then brilliant alphabets of code
our dim eyes could not decipher.
We tried reciting poetry—
the Ode to Autumn, Adam's Curse—
but lost those lines within a buzz
of half-remembered table talk,
psalms and homilies, slogans, names,
a palimpsest inscribed in chalk,
erased by time, revised.

                    I said
Everything's ending, isn't it?
Each day subsides a little soon,
we hardly notice fall until
full dark envelops us by five,
a lid closed firm and cool. Your lawn's
alive, a dance where predator
and prey ignite small wars, are killed,

or live and fly away somewhere.
Do bugs have souls? Do we? Recall
that physics principle from school:
energy can't begin or end.
We pass in time from form to form,
containers for a glow not ours.
(Stray fireflies flickered on and off.)
Whatever faith's conditional
reward or punishment, we're light
at last, electrics passed between
synapses, until the power
cuts one off and fires another.

You said
            But that's not proof of souls;
in fact it's bullshit, blasphemy
to some, at best inspired by wine.
We aren't lights strung for holidays,
or ohms, or fireflies, Jesus Christ.
What about our wars where millions
died: were they easy come, easy
go to hell, souls transformed to sperm
and egg and born anew to shine?
Souls can't be proved by physics class;
they're human constructs, distinguish
us from them, the great unwashed we
won't share heaven with.

                              I replied
Say God's a brain imagining itself,

okay? It knows its weakest place,
so defends with emissaries:
ghosts and angels, flying objects,
meteors of viral fossils,
invasive dreams we can't resist
describing—things and presences
chipped from the strange original
we fear or doubt but don't deny.
If there were nothing, we'd exist
alone, vacuum-packed electrons
spinning on this stone's beginning
journey, whose end we'll never know.
And I don't want to live that way.

The fireflies had been dark a while.
You sat quiet; I felt you cry
a bit, then choke it back with wine.
What's wrong? Nothing. Did I say—? No.
It's just . . . I'm scared I might be sick.
There's something wrong inside my skin.
I cough and cough, it's like a hinge
deep down my throat that won't unstick.
My boyfriend says he's tested fine
but—sometimes I think he's lying.

A wind came up, nearby a door
slammed shut, creaked open, slammed again.
The dark enlarged, a space no light
could fill nor prayer diminish.
Behind a calm low cloud the moon's

reflected glow illumined us:
an absent presence, softer than
fluorescence but as clinical,
abstract, answering no questions,
examining without pity,
salvation none of its business.

Twitched in the forsythia,
Hooked my eye and held it
Like a hackled lure cast out
From eroding sills of light.

Too bright
For that late hour, the bush
Ignited flower by flower to
Furnace-roar and glare where the bird

Alit, delicate.
Slender beak, sleek
Head cocked, tricked out in black
Array, he mimed the butler's clock-

Work of deft bows and plucked
One ladybug (*fly away home*)
From an amber cluster
Suppering on dew, then flew

Into the moon,
A throne away from home,
The bug his jeweled crown,
My eye his perilune.

CEREMONY

The snake lay in state like a king
Slabbed on limestone, overlooking
The river he hunted and ruled.
His mail glittered copper and gold
With dew, for the morning was cool,
That pooled into watering holes
On the pitted stone. It seemed
He would rise when the damp bier steamed
Like a pyre catching flame—the wood
Hushed its breath, the sleek mice he'd kill
Held still beneath roots—but a wind
Bearing five small white butterflies
Blew the fire out; they unfastened
His skin and stripped him down to size
And, firm slender mouths probing, mined
The warm hive of the inner core.
Vanished, as if they never were.

THE HIVE

Totemic head of mud and ash compressed,
Crumbling above bones, bird skulls bleached pristine,
   Fossil trilobite and fern, pinned
      Butterflies crisp as toast,
      Chrysalis and starfish—
   Shards of a world I gleaned and fixed,

The basement museum proof of Beyond.
   Kids drawn from the neighborhood's nooks
Would quiet, as if taking communion.
      Mom let them stroke relics
      Like the blind seeking sight
   While she led the way through the dark.

   Egghead collector, slouching shy
      To hide my eagerness
(For this routine was pitched to win me friends),
      I'd wait for her barker's canny
      Prompt: "Son, remember when
You found the hive?" Wedged beneath an eave,

Our home's deepest and most angled,
Its location seemed an evil
    Mark, proof of inner rot.
    Its swarm was power raw,
An open cable; summer thrummed, our street
Shook with sound like a child's glassed-in tableau.

    Soon sidewalks crackled, tires went lame,
        Dogs were driven insane.
The neighbors'd had it and told us so:
Property values were going to hell.
        They had their rights, you know;
        They were frightened for the children.

We couldn't burn the thing, so intimate
        Its hold was on the house,
        Swelling with a tumor's ease.
The local handyman wanted no part.
        Dad laddered up to diagnose:
        "This is a job for your mother!"

    At dusk the neighborhood came by
    To gawk. The hive sucked back its swarm
        Like a jar its genie.
"You'd think this was religion," Mom chortled,
        Relishing her new fame.
"Guess it doesn't get this good on Sunday."

Twin poison aerosols in hand
She began her climb, paused halfway, took aim.
Through pale mist the hive writhed as if in pain.
Larvae sizzled from it,
Though two or three survivors sawed
Confusedly away.

For days it hung, a hieroglyph for fear.
Silence recaptured sway;
The neighbors' whispering rustled the air.
Our name became a hex to say.
Birds furled on the powerlines.
At last Dad hacked it down—

Where now, its dominion the world's old bones,
The hive blackens in our display,
Smelling of pesticide.
All the kids are far gone,
Escaped; their parents have moved on or died.
Home to visit one holiday,

Spying through glass, I watch Mom clean downstairs.
Thick with webs, the museum seems
A long-abandoned lair
Where husks sipped dry of life are strewn.
The vacuum's muffled roar diminishes,
Cut—before the hive she

Bows a slow minute, as if in penance
To that raging idol she had silenced
  One summer evening, years ago.
  Sweet sepulchre, you whose children
    Woke to die inside you,
    Return my lonely one.

PUFFBALL

Upon the beach one dawn this fist-sized globe,
pale green, no root or shell. Dead animal
the sea coughed up, unborn original,
rare alien? It cottoned to my robe.
Inside, I scraped and probed to no avail.
Soft-fleshed but firm, the thing resisted me;
no book or lens unsheathed its history,
cell delicate but impenetrable.
By night my guest swelled red with mystery:
a head, its fissured eyes and lips compressed
and bulged, as if some roaring laugh was blessed
by praying hands that gripped its blistered glee.
Next day I woke on fire, my skin a nest,
my veil of seeds shimmering in conquest.

All night the storm's electric hand touched down
around the island, shivering my bed.
By dawn rank evidence: the sand a gown
ripped back, a runneled grave of maidenhead
some god disgusted by excess had strewn.
Gulls screamed and strutted proud upon the dead,
old emperors incarnate with ruin,
their courtiers flies; abuzz with praise they fed.
I walked among stiff eyeless fish, pocked shells
of flesh exposed, my arms a cross, immune,
like one stray revenant escaping hell's
domain for human shores—our round commune—
who finds the houses dark, whole cities charnel,
no one to welcome me and none to tell.

There are countries that don't see the water
we grow fairways with; or burn off acres
into fairways we might come to play on,
spreading dollar tips behind like stale bread
to guide the way back. Parrots, if you pay
in unmarked currencies of bread, that will
intone their keepers' names like prophecies
of thunder. Then tuck sleek green heads away.
People who, grinding teeth in sleep (you hear
the rasp of stones churning down to sand), wake
to pour coffee, trim fruit with a dull blade,
lay the plates like islands on the bay-blue
table where you work, write long letters home,
read the mail that comes by boat, and listen.

For what? How easy to misinterpret
the ocean's rumbling as your own hunger,
deep in the gut; to find in flowers' names
an alien hieroglyph for vengeance;
to hear the island hustling closer in
the insects' hidden buzzsaws, day and night.
Listen. Whole forests topple while you sleep.
Lean shadows, liberated from their trees

like an army of Ariels, advance
over the beachhead asking *Why? How long?*
And, where a shark cuts its phosphorescent
signature through surf, the ocean answers
Soon. Here in this calm haven you are king.
Live long and you will govern everything.

On summer's porch, we sated men
chat with our dogs, the evening
sliding easy as a beer.
Now and then a wife leans out
to say hello, or children
come for goodnight kisses, shy as deer.
But this is men's work, this low talk,
these eyes checking off the chalk
lines of property, ours to keep
if we will.
       So when an animal
somewhere cries out terrified,
or approaching headlights blindside
the buckled timber on the fence,
the rewards of vigilance
seem so frail that one jogger
grips our hearts, and the neighbor's
inbred hellhound stirs from slumber,
ready to fight.
       But stays put,
for men find ways to hold it all
in place—a phrase, common handle
to fix the shirtless stranger:

Hey buddy   *Take it slow, Joe*

generic names for our shared nightmare.
The footsteps pound on, passing, past.
Lapped by the world that once chased us
with promises, guzzling its dust,
we are the sons our fathers
lit cigars to welcome home.
Echoes of their voices
call across the avenue,
reminding us what might have been
had it been ours to do,
now mingle with the high-pitched thrive
of cricket wings, rasping from the space
they rent, but do not own.

Our foundling fathers named with irony,
Perhaps intentional, given hindsight.
Eagle's Nest, River Valley, Sunset Height,
Hillandale, Mountain Lakes, Serenity:
Developments where packaged memory
Evokes places bulldozed to inhabit.
When God and government cooperate
Our garden profits, faith's a money tree.

We moved here, urban refugees who bought
The brochure pitch—no crime, low tax, few blacks
(though no one says that last aloud). Relax.
The better life comes cheaper than you thought.
Lanes are named for fallen trees, cul-de-sacs
For Indians whose tribes our fathers fought.
Two cops patrol: their beaming juggernaut
Illuminates our lawns and furtive acts,

Our petty crimes against this paradise
Of civic pride. It's easy to get lost,
Bewildered by familiar friendly hosts—
Each home's identical mirage of lights
And sculpted shrubs, a steal at twice the price.

Kids often wander in, oblivious,
Then start to wail, as if we're hungry ghosts
Who've downed their folks and carved the bones to dice.

The idea's to recreate a childhood
Common ground, dominion of Dad and Mom
To which watchful doormats offer Welcome.
Glassed within idealized tableaux, our good
Money buys perfection; still, we fear some
Stranger guest, pedophile or drifter god
Who manufactures similes of home.
Before we know what's hit us we'll be food.

It's odd: the lawns, turf flush against high curbs,
Discourage any neighborly forays,
The sugar loans and elegant soirees
We've meant to host, but never found the nerve.
No walks, so no one does; we drive the curves
Of dead-end lanes, wave semaphore *Okays*,
Mouth *Hi!* and *How are you!* against the day
We're forced to meet and find we can't converse.

Safe from sin we conjure local devils:
Sprites that char the barbecue, rev the car
In crowds of kids at play, transmute sugar
Into salt, wine to vinegar to swill.
Garage doors yawn like graves awaiting war.
Our dogs are paranoid, sniffing evil
Everywhere; their howls announce arrivals
We can't discern or hear but know are there:

Our fathers, maybe, or the things they shot,
Hacked down, ploughed then plucked, fucked up and over,
Raped, infected, sued, drove undercover,
Extinguished for the greater good, forgot.
Our neighborhood's generic Camelot
Makes the past a mortgage we can cover
By paying down old debts with new, a knot
Binding us to God and one another.

This summer night reclines, voluptuous.
Our porch lights beckon moth-like children home
To sleep's cocoon, protective catacomb.
Kneeling, they ask for apparent purpose,
Care's evidence, a well-provisioned womb.
Tomorrow they're reborn, cauled and viscous
With thick dreams, clawing eyes so light—God's tusk—
Can penetrate them, begetting wisdom.

Does God select whose praise most entertains,
Which plea to taste? Our minister demurs;
He doesn't countenance particulars.
Yet we distinguish *human* from *humane*—
Both suggesting mercy's obligation,
That final *e* conferring sinecure,
Our right to finish off some thing (a run-down
Squirrel, say) whose pain we can't endure.

Sometimes I pray without much confidence,
My hedge against decline eventual,
A prudent measure, not confessional—
Like latching doors and windows firm against

Intruders. TV's companionable,
Its lullaby a rhyme of violence
I channel surf to cleanse my guilty sense
Of privilege, voyeur at a funeral.

The news tonight: two friends are suicides,
Teenagers wrapped around each other's waist.
Their Last Embrace—the anchorwoman's face
Mimes sympathy, frown lines and fluid eyes.
Neighbors offer fingerpointing bromides:
This used to be a paradise, this place.
What's wrong with us? The screen disintegrates,
My choice. A pixel light, then black. Outside

Our street's fluorescent as a lab, the glow
Of faux gas lamps and floodlights dimming stars,
Moon a would-be clinical observer
Blinded by reflection. Timid shadows
Fledge like deer emerging from a grove no
Longer here; they pause to test the air.
A birch or two hang on, gentle elders
Pampered toward extinction, white hollow

Husks watered now and then by Maintenance,
Last stand before their end. Intermittent
Bug trap zaps and sizzles keep us solvent,
Fireflies and bats and luna moths entranced
And fried: No Trespassing. Inheritance
Demands that we be ever vigilant,
To keep with gun or fence the providence
Our fathers brought forth on this continent.

OVERLOOK

At the overlook decreed as scenic
my eye watched autumn burn without much care
like TV fires they linger on to pique
you for the sports. The view confirmed our state's
opinion of itself—July-warm lakes
gave up their misty ghosts to cooler air,
sun lanced the slope, a cloud's obliging cleft
dispersed its rays to praiseworthy effect—
but I stood black and dry as wood engaged
by gypsy moths, our paradise's plague.
Their winged meanness fluttered loose within me.
No reason why—if you're expecting one,
forget it: this isn't confessional.
I wished to rot and be done with it all.

But my skin held form; ramose mannequin,
weathering every season's boom or bust,
I became a local landmark famous
for my pluck. Postcards of my silhouette
gnarled against the sunset were big business.
Like vultures children preened in my embrace.
Soon the state roped me off, nailed up a plaque,
a hydrant nearby in case lightning struck.

Blaspheming freely, I prayed for such luck.
Nothing doing, said God, our governor's
friend—but an angel escaped his domain:
A wandering goldfinch, candle alive,
lit each sere branch tip it touched in my name.
Whatever killed me took wing from the flame.

SPARK

The secret fire,
The fire that costs,
The fire you kill to keep,

Not the conflagration
Lit without intent,
The accidental
Ember that chars a mountain
Black, then suffocates,

But the tended single
Flame, prepared for—
A circle cleared of scrub
And raked, new earth
Damp around it—

Begins as appetite, the body's
Craving for specific
Tastes at timely intervals,

Then passes over
Into hunger, a dull
Round stone

Distending the gut
So no bread can pass, no meat
Satisfy nor liquid soothe,

A painful swell that shifts
Like a child never to be born,
So hands fold over it and
Press, to hold it still;

Until one day that stone is
Struck hard,
Fault lines shivered to its core

By a blade that might be anything—
A pale trout glimpsed, then lost,
Shadow on new snow, a sentence
Spoken quiet in a crowd—

So the stone of hunger
Sparks, hands that cradled it
Now scrabble fuel to feed

A flame that burns but does not
Consume the stone, that heat
At once your famine and your sustenance.

The stars are up, their easy rhymes
wing down and strut like paradigms
of pigeons feeding by a fount.
Constellations mount—
Arcturus red, Orion letting out
his belt another notch of light
to accommodate the night's
expanding girth.
                Here on earth
the story crazes: two local kids
rape a girl and leave her for dead.
One fifteen, the other twelve,
freckled Huck and Tom come back by way of hell.
Where can you put your hatred? blurts
the anchorman, then cuts.

Morning's paper frames the pair.
True from distance, up close
their faces disappear
to dots, black holes
devouring gravity and time.
Just so a small town anywhere:
from the stars, our paths down here

must seem reflected in a shallow pool—
avenues lit and clear, the surface whole—
but when the banks erode, brim
like bogs with mist and buried men,
what lamp can penetrate, or traveler span?

EAVESDROPPER

I couldn't help but overhear
your desert whispers—assumption
wished for in that prayer so fierce
no god but ours would answer it.
These days there's hardly anyone
who'll listen without recompense,
some tradeoff you negotiate,
damp coiling secret you can't house
but must, to disentangle yours.
We all want crime or private sin
to mark us with the human touch,
black thumbprint smudging every brow:
I confess. Perfection's suspect;
like cops we test its alibi,
exposing inconsistencies
until the story's paradise
erodes, the rattler's fangs unsheathe.
Who wouldn't doubt? Even TV's
prophecies seem manufactured,
plague and genocide tricks of light,
the news a stage where victims' moms
obligingly collapse on cue.
You beg to leave, the great escape—

ideally without pain, you'd ride
upwelling thermals like a gull,
gaze down upon our planet cell—
to where your audience has heard
it all, supernal bartender
who never gives advice or rings
the tab, just polishes and nods
and waits, in case you want to talk.

SNAPPER

Ours devoured red worms,
Beef pellets; stupefied,
Lay swamped in shallow muck,
Eyes white with cataracts,
Old woman's lined neck
Groping out at mealtime,
Gut swollen against glass.
Precise hinged jaws
Unlocked, closed firm as wirecutters.
Would snap pencils when pricked.
Buried in a card box.

So, when something like a stone
Shifts near shore—not the stone's
Position, but its shape,
As if a shadow
Assumed mass around it—
The lakebed's easeful food chain
Rattles; surface swirls
Mark where minnows were.
And worse: reaching for a coin
He'd dropped, one kid lost a joint
To the shadow's appetite.

In sleep I've rowed through swamp,
Fish strung like heavy jewels
From my chain; awakened
Trembling, their shredded skins
Proof of an invisible
Core that swallows,
Unappeasable.
Our pet: it had no name.
Bored, we'd poke it, asking
Are you hungry yet?

Here things come to die, are discarded when
superiors decide enough's enough,
won't pay to haul or bury on their own.
Replenished by the roadside sewer drain
its water glistens after rain, runoff
inching a dominion out of ruin,
frog for idol, dragonfly for seraph.
Beer cans coral-bright, bald tire drowned mid-yawn,
coins some ironist had wished his life on—
these, and the stray cat's litter bagged to suf-
focate, road kills shoveled in, a wagon's
worth of snakes snuffed from one home's undercroft,
the mad dog shot: *Forget* their epitaph.
Driving by we gasp, roll the windows shut;
still, it insinuates our every breath
with all we cannot learn the meaning of.
We crave its mysteries, its lover's hiss.
Asleep each night we drink its deepest kiss.

HOLIDAY CAKE

Christmas week
Paul would come, circling the block
In a maroon Buick
Minus its muffler,
Hard coughs to clear its throat of phlegm.
Starting around 11 a.m.
He'd visit door to door, hugging the curb
Like a paperboy, crunching furtive
Through the snow with
His gift:

Wrapped in foil,
Moist to the touch, substantial,
Studded with raisins, dates,
Candied apricots,
Sugared almonds, chunks of walnuts,
Cherries dipped in rum—so pungent
We stored it in the china cabinet
For a year, basted in cinnamon
To moderate
The taste.

Our parents
Would greet him, invite him in

For eggnog, but Paul sensed
We thought him odd—
Shabby down jacket, this mission
Performed yearly, no expectation
Of return—and declined. The year he died
We shouted carols at his doorstep
Until he showed,
Gaunt, pleased

For such friends.
The next Christmas we sat down
To supper, devouring
Slabs of lamb, plump peas
In butter, mashed potatoes, wine:
Too-plentiful preliminaries
To the sweet feast baked and simply given
One year ago. Remembering Paul,
We said a grace
And ate.

GUEST STAR

Something coming down at night,
Roar of metal wheels on stone
A covenant unto us
Inside our house. Then ripping
Intermittent cracks of air,
Like Mom's laundry on the line
Much amplified, enormous.
Hushed before the TV's eye
We heard plaster walls compress
Against what force wanted in.

Dad kept rising from his chair
To squint through windows: Nothing.
Streetlights globed our neighborhood,
Fluorescent cell where nothing
Subdivided or decayed.
TV didn't register
An interruptive tremor;
Bright familiar comedies
Resolved, laugh tracks unafraid.
Then the dog began to howl

Like crazy. We all inhaled.
Should you call someone? Mom said.

Where were the authorities?
Surely they already knew,
Would muster guns and sirens,
Action for tomorrow's news.
Dad got up to look again.
The stars seemed dim, enshadowed
By a larger guest between.
I doubt anyone's in charge.

NIGHT TENNIS

Asleep, my mother startles into flight,
ungainly bird, all beak and hollow bone,
helmeted in gauze to swathe the surgeon's
burr-hole signature. Rising over town
she hopes no pimpled scout astronomer
has focused in, she'll never live it down,
Housewife Jailed for Corrupting a Minor.
From this height the courts are glowing jewels,
jade carved with secret hieroglyphs and lit,
but as she settles—banking arms like wings,
her gown a handy parachute—the lines
make sense, an alphabet unlocks its code.
Three friends she hasn't seen in years arrive
in chrome-finned cars, their bodies young again.
The game begins. At first erratic,
hacking shots she used to make look simple,
she finds her legs and arms are functional,
no longer paralyzed. Her skills return;
covering the court like an animal
she probes for corners, creating angles
her friends applaud—four women without men
to hog the net and butcher overheads,

enjoying the night, companionably
calling honest lines, calling across them
Just wide or *Deep* or, when my mother's lob
lofts seemingly to join the stars but top-
spins down, down and in: *Beauty, ah beauty.*

A front's cloud edge advances from the north,
before it blue, the climate our state praised
these months, the sort of sun you angle for
in church, negotiating sin away.
Now wind's the whisper of apocalypse,
the weatherman's chiseled grin collapses.
Our reservoirs decline. History's ghost
haunts every channel: drought remedial
to flood, illegal graves revealed, a skull
the moral camera zooms in upon,
then fades to black.

                  Will the sun undo us,
so fierce our shadows cower in disguise?
(The forests flame with autumn realized,
lawns peel like hair from chemotherapy.)
Will skin balms and deodorants shield us
or serve as shrouds that we are buried in?
Thick with rain the clouds plane down, electrics
distantly colliding; eyes scorched by light
we pause at windows, gather on the porch.
You tiptoe out, afraid to break the spell,
hands like leaves before you cupped in prayer.
Any minute now, it'll be okay.
You look back for someone to agree with.

When the first tree toppled no one
Heard, hence no sound, no evidence.
    An event measured by
    Silent shiftings toward:
Near canopies annexing light's
Unbroken shaft, the forest floor
    Alive with listeners
Hustling to claim the catacomb
As home, entropy their mansion.
    Like great hearts giving way
    Tree after tree collapsed,
Roots parting with the start of shots,
Unmistakable, but offstage—
    In another country—
    So easily ignored.
"A bacterium," someone bluffed.
"No, the rain." "No, the tree itself."
Philosophy denied the sound
If we declined to witness it.
The faculties of eye and ear
Diminished with our habitat
    As the plague of silence
    Spread wild like fire in drought,
Though we huddled in the city's

Drone of power and blinding glass,
    A throne inviolate.
To hear now would acknowledge then
That tree's demise, its colony's
    Ascendancy of sense.
Forests are falling all around
Without a sound, no sound at all.

A creature without consequence or fame:
  No big plans were hindered by it,
    No native religion
   Claimed its tutelary spirit
Or found the sacred in the species' flame.

It was simply in the way and gave way
  Unaware, females dying down
    Until five males remained
   To echo their own antiphon,
Priests made to offer common eulogy.

Its habitat, a marsh in Florida,
  Abutted Cape Canaveral,
    Launch pad of our nation's
   Hopes in cones of flames and metal
Hurtling toward God, the grand idea

That justifies whatever's sacrificed.
  Not news unless the last male died;
    Then, a minor headline,
   Regretful quote from one who tried
To breed it from captivity's demise.

Not worth noticing, a brown, six-inch bird,
   Forgettable by tomorrow
      But for the lovely name—
    The pure dusky seaside sparrow—
We gave it, as a token of our word.

The mind alone
Hoards small familiars
Pleasing for the thrum
They summon, when touched.
The humble mussel's
Heft fills the black lake
Rippling beneath fog,
Surface imageless
Above deep structures.
Shard of mica rubbed
Ignites the sun
That burns the fog off
Clean, like stripping skin,
The lake exposed in
Bone and tendon,
Bottom stone and weed.
From a fallen leaf
Intricate of vein
Rise thick woods gamy
With the smell of rain,
The trees' reflections
Cut into the lake
Like cathedral glass.

Now the mind conjures
An apparition
In its own image—
Shadow cast by shade,
Breath inside the wind's
Wide exhalation—
To survey its realm,
Mark its boundaries
And its species name.
The eidolon roams
Listening for song,
Snap of twig, rustle
Beneath fallen leaves
Or swirl from the lake's
Hungry undercroft.
But the mind alone
Cannot fledge out bird
From frail feather's quill,
Nor trout from single
Iridescent scale,
Cannot from fern seed
Populate the woods.
Climbing highest oak,
Sieving bottom muck
For another life,
The eidolon finds
Barren paradise,
Raw fields pecked by light's
Hard beak, motes of dust

To companion it
And wind to whisper
The covenant of
What abandoned it:
Wish, to remember;
Echo or forget.

SURVIVED BY

Everyone you knew is gone,
died or fled without a word,
rooms you shared now graves, open
questions never answered.

Were you loved? Or unaware,
obliged to money's office,
too busy to attend where
word or touch gave notice.

Did you love? In your fashion—
time permitting, when required.
Convenience married passion
as dirt reduces fire

to dampened ash, charred circle
walkers find and wonder who
ignited this initial;
how many years ago,

and let die unattended,
temple without genius,
some ceremony ended
here, nothing to discuss.

TURNING A KALEIDOSCOPE

This stupid lawn chair's hell, a prison cell;
noon-hot plastic crosshatch stripes my butt
as if I've sinned, as if the stroke's my fault.
I'd rather die than linger as some skull,
hollowed-out and bleached, a lab's Exhibit
A: here's what happens when you're curious,
know-it-all who doubts the larger purpose.
People say thank God I'm alive: Bullshit.
If God's awake he's laughing at his joke,
comedian with teeth that snapped my neck.

I'm planted here to ripen in the sun,
exotic vegetable, head swathed in gauze.
No one remembers I'm still who I was—
a little worse for wear, but not undone.
A woman, not a child to patronize
or pet who slobbers on command for food.
It's hard to listen without seeming rude.
I'm sick of being prayed for and questioned,
my therapy the neighbors' dinner talk.
To shut them up I have to learn to walk.

Turning my kaleidoscope, memories
ghost back in shadow play where I'm the star.

Bits of colored glass between two mirrors
opposite, a plastic tube—yet beauty's
in each turn, as light becomes cathedral.
I amuse myself for hours, aiming where
the spirit moves, from bright to darker aisles.
The solid world dissolves, material
transformed to atoms dancing toward repose.
My house's brick unfolds, a layered rose.

The stroke I can't recall—just sudden dark,
cool bathroom floor beneath my head an ease
so comforting I slid near sleep's release . . .
then NO. Some meanness jerked me wide awake,
pacemaker my heart drummed double-time to,
proof I still was, my voice from far thrown back.
You haven't lived till rage comes over you.
When someone else walked in I tried to say
my savior word, but my mouth wouldn't work.
"Okay," they answered, "it'll be okay."

Supposedly a tumor knocked me out.
The CAT scan lit some shadow on my brain,
darkness in the labyrinth, sly circuit-
breaker. Like flipping off a switch, it cut
my nerves' electric net. As the surgeon
touched his pointer here and here, a question
troubled me to ask, What if nothing's there?
No monster in the maze? The surgeon smiled;
he "shared in my concern," but he was sure.
My brain had nursed a beast he had to kill.

The night before my trial I said goodbye,
though not aloud—bad luck to summon
Death, that most eligible bachelor.
Head shaved, gowned in white, I felt like a bride
alright, a milk-fed sacrificial one.
My husband made a joke, snapped my picture
just in case: if I survived he'd tease me
without mercy. The kids tried not to cry;
among thick flowers and balloons galore
I must have seemed a grinning skull, the lie

behind what facts they understood of life.
A nurse came in with pills to help me rest.
They left, kisses and *I love you*'s their best
medicine. Last thing I remember
the hall's red Exit flickered on and off.
When I awakened, bright sun lined the air—
rays like spread fingers, visible with dust.
Each grain gleamed gold so intricate I knew:
Alive, I'm still alive. I'd made it through
the maze and left my monster raging there.

That tumor was mirage, a machine ghost.
I guess the surgeon felt compelled to boast
and craved my scalp as proof of victory.
He said his technique was impeccable;
he displayed my clean burr-holes to any-
one who'd look. Hospitals are filled with ghouls
so I drew quite a crowd, a freak for real.

I should have charged admission. Malpractice
can't describe what that doctor did. In hell
I hope he burns and I'm the arsonist.

Returning home, I learned again old skills
we take for granted, our rich kids' birthright.
My steel wheelchair seemed punishment, not aid;
it glared ferociously, inanimate
but strong. The damned thing gave me nightmare chills.
My husband folded it beneath our bed.
Therapy's no picnic: you're drenched in sweat
by simple things, just getting off the floor's
a triumph. I yanked my numb leg forward,
again, again, cursing God as I wept,

so frustrated and tired I thought to die
would be relief. Screw the medication:
three little pills, my daily remedy,
that thinned my blood and tranquilized my brain.
In health's disguise they made me Frankenstein,
the perfect Wife and Mom, trained to obey.
My husband worked, kids went to school; alone
I learned to think and talk again, to clean
and cook on one hand and leg, alibi
my hurt with smiles. I could pass as human.

Still, some perceived death's pupil in my glance—
usually their own demon, what they feared most
possessing me. One by one old friends lost

touch: a get-well card, a call, then silence.
That cruelty would make your hair go white.
When you're disabled you're anonymous;
people speak not *with* but *at* you, a pet
they kiss or curse, whatever they require.
Some weirdos touch me with dry lips, then cross
their chests, like I'm a patron saint for hire—

can you believe? Others like their details
gory, confront me on the street to ask,
"What's wrong with you?" I mime bewilderment,
eyebrows raised, shoulders shrugged "Is something wrong?"
They stride away like something's on their tails,
uncontrolled and strange, virus in a masque.
You'd think a stroke's contagious, evidence
of moral rot that only prayer can dredge.
I don't mind church if that's what turns you on;
selfish piety sets my teeth on edge.

My god dwells outdoors, not in bread or wine,
campy props we use to quiet children.
Imagination animates, the touch
of fingertip to tip connecting each
of us to something large and alien.
It doesn't have our little fates in mind.
It doesn't have a mind—no television
tuned to man's soap opera. In the wind,
the dirt, the seeds that rise to sun it dwells
apart from us, forever parallel.

Within this kaleidoscope my garden
blooms anew, colors flaring on a wheel.
I dreamed it in the hospital, alone
at night, when visitors had long since gone.
It hovered midair, mirage surreal,
its arbors and damp secrets paradise.
How many mornings did I awaken
parched and weeping, locked outside that promise?
To enter I would have to die or heal;
the former would be easier. I chose.

Some months had passed when I came home—by then
the garden was an ugly wilderness,
weed-choked, gnawed by bugs, nearly left for dead.
Stalks rotted where they fell like corpses'
hair and skeletons. I began to bed,
seeding and pruning, my spade a jawbone
slaying parasites, yanking up slick roots.
My cold nerves tingled as if played upon.
A ragged bird perched near and cocked its head.
It's dumb to say but something underfoot

flowed through me like a current of desire.
Now crocuses burn low with spring's first thaw;
igniting branch by branch, forsythia
flare at night so moths whirl around their fire.
Come June pink roses cargo the arbors
whose nooks delay avid bees past curfew.
Tiger lilies, chrysanthemum and phlox,

petunia, gladiola, iris stalks
too delicate to trim—my touch renewed
their lives as they had welcomed mine. Thank you.

My leg's returning too, nerve mending nerve,
a spiderweb alive and delicate.
The healing hurts—it's like a match has lit
each filament's slow fuse from hip to toe—
but I can feel again. Small things: the curve
of wind along my calf, caress of grass
dawn-wet with dew, my husband's palm's hello.
More than anything I missed the compass
touch provides, that mutual laying on
of hands confirming your true direction.

Such mystery surrounds us, yet we doze
before the TV screen, almighty Oz
we worship without knowing why, afraid
to live without incessant background noise.
Most creatures need to listen or be flayed;
we prey upon ourselves, our senses tuned
within, engendering pursuers there.
I've learned more from animal than human
things of God (the catch-all name our prayers
address whenever something isn't "fair")—

learned, but never known. For the why of it
escapes my grasp, the hidden pattern shifts;
like broken glass the world kaleidoscopes

on me, evolving into stranger shapes.
Have you ever seen at evening's sway
the sparrows rise and settle, rise again?
One bird seems to guide them, signaling when
it's time to feed and when to fly away.
I've watched and watched, and still I can't decide
if that bird leads, or if it's somehow led.

The undersides of things are ticklish:
palms, bellies, backs of knees,
surfaces scored with nerves,
concave, convex, any place
you lift or turn to touch.
A stone dead but for its lichen
thrives underneath, a mine
of wriggling kin. Too much
sexy stuff for some (exclaiming Oh!
they slam the lid down, screw it tight);
for others—okay, for me—hope:
that any grave might hide delight,
that every shape must have its mate,
the counter-curve to true it up.
So you're shy, yet your secret tongue—
doesn't it?—savors this note's envelope.

ACKNOWLEDGMENTS

The author gratefully acknowledges the following publications, in which these poems first appeared: *The Atlantic*: "The Country of Perfect Weekends." *Boulevard*: "Spoils." *Confrontation*: "Clipping an Obituary" and "The Vantage Point." *Flyway*: "Halloween." *The Formalist*: "Puffball." *Gettysburg Review*: "The Apparitioners," "Holiday Cake," and "Star Rhyme." *Kenyon Review*: "Turning a Kaleidoscope." *New York Quarterly*: "Voiceover." *Poet & Critic*: "Spark." *Poetry*: "Gully," "Narcissus," "Thaw," and "Totenwald." *Prairie Schooner*: "October Rose" and "Yours Truly." *Seneca Review*: "The Hive." *Shenandoah*: "Overlook," "Snapper," and "Talus Slope." *Southwest Review*: "Alphabet," "An Open Letter," "The Covered Well," "Porch Talk," and "To Be Opened in the Event." *Sycamore Review*: "Hey Buddy." In addition, "At Dusk, the Catbird," "Ceremony," and "Pinion" first appeared in *The Secret Alphabet*, a chapbook published as part of the Sea Cliff Press New Poets Series.

GEORGE WITTE

has published poems in *The Atlantic, Gettysburg Review, Kenyon Review, Poetry, Southwest Review,* and elsewhere. He was awarded *Poetry's* Frederick Bock Prize for a group of poems, and received a fellowship from the New Jersey State Council on the Arts/Department of State. For twenty years he has worked in book publishing, as an editor for St. Martin's Press, publisher of Picador USA, and now as editor in chief of St. Martin's Press. He lives with his wife and two daughters in Glen Rock, New Jersey.

MILLVILLE PUBLIC LIBRARY
MILLVILLE, New Jersey

————

1. Unless otherwise noted, books are issued for three weeks.

2. A fine of five cents a day is charged on each book kept overtime.

3. The borrower is held responsible for all books drawn on his card and all fines accruing on the same.

GAYLORD R